Team
Terrificus

TIPS & TECHNIQUES WITH
THE FRUIT OF THE SPIRIT FOR
LEADERS' & MEMBERS' SUCCESS

Team

Terrificus

Lynn M. Hayden

Tips & Techniques With
The Fruit of the Spirit for Leaders'
& Members' Success

OTHER BOOKS BY THE AUTHOR

Dancing For Him

Dance, Dance,Dance!

Processionals, Props, and Pageantry

Dancers' Devotional Calendar

Dance In The Church, What's the Pointe?

Creative Worship

Prophetic Dance

Divine Choreography

Please visit our web site:
www.dancingforhim.com
And go to our on line book store for more details...

TEAM TERRIFICUS

Team: *"A group of people working together in a coordinated effort; to join in a cooperative activity; people who individually subordinate personal aspirations and work in a coordinated effort with other members of a group, or team, in striving for a common goal."* [1*]

Terrificus: *"To frighten; causing great fear or dismay; unusually great, intense, severe, unusually fine, admirable, enjoyable; a general term of approval."*

Contents

DEDICATION

To my very special worship dance mentors: Caroline Hinton, Linda Jones, and Missy Marcinkowski. Over the years, they taught me a great deal about dance team leadership by truly exemplifying the fruit of the Spirit.

Introduction

Galatians 5:16 – 26 "I say then: Walk in the Spirit, and you shall not fulfill the lust of the flesh. For the flesh lusts against the Spirit, and the Spirit against the flesh; and these are contrary to one another, so that you do not do the things that you wish. But if you are led by the Spirit, you are not under the law. Now the works of the flesh are evident, which are: adultery, fornication, uncleanness, lewdness, idolatry, sorcery, hatred, contentions, jealousies, outbursts of wrath, selfish ambitions, dissentions, heresies, envy, murders, drunkenness, revelries, and the like; of which I tell you beforehand, just as I also told you in time past, that those who practice such things will not inherit the kingdom of God. But the **fruit of the Spirit is love, joy, peace, patience, kindness, goodness, faithfulness, gentleness, self-control.** *Against such there is no law. And those who are Christ's have crucified the flesh with its passions and desires. If we live in the Spirit, let us also walk in the Spirit. Let us not become conceited, provoking one another, envying one another."* 2*

Team: "A group of people working together in a coordinated effort; to join in a cooperative activity; people who individually subordinate personal aspirations and work in a coordinated effort with other members of a group, or team, in striving for a common goal.

Terrificus: "To frighten; causing great fear or dismay; unusually great, intense, severe, unusually fine, admirable, enjoyable; a general term of approval."

Dance teams and leaders are called to practice and grow the fruit of the Spirit, so that when expressive worship or presentations are done, the purity of the Holy Spirit is exemplified and not the works of the flesh. We have a responsibility as Spirit filled believers to build character. The fruit of the Spirit and good *character* should be as evident as His gifts that are shown through our *char*ismatic activity (arts presentations).

It is my desire and God's design to combine both the fruit of the Spirit and basic team concepts in this booklet . When a group of people **(team)** *"individually subordinate personal aspirations and work in a coordinated effort with other members of a team in striving for a common goal",* they become **terrificus (terrific).** While causing great fear or dismay toward the enemy of our souls, their movements become intense, unusually great, and severe in the heavenly realm. As a unified front, who attain victory over the defeated one, they become unusually fine, admirable, and enjoyable. In order for this to be accomplished, this *terrific team* must walk in the Spirit or walk in line with the Holy Spirit's plan by exercising His fruit. It is only the Holy Spirit who can produce this fruit in us. Whereas the rotten works of the flesh may easily be accomplished by our own hand. When a team member truly allows the Spirit of God to totally control their life, the plurality and the manifestation of the singular word "fruit" will genuinely be exemplified. How much more powerful may the anointing be when a whole team lays down the plural works of the flesh (a stench and unpleasant taste to God and man) and demonstrate the singular, sweet fruit of the Spirit?

I've divided the booklet into three parts: Our Attitude toward God and Team, Social Relationships On and Off the Team, and Principles Guiding Conduct. Upon closer observation of the fruit of the Spirit, we can see that the nine graces could be divided in thirds, respectively.

Over the years, while serving both as a dance team member and a leader, and after listening to and counseling many other dance leaders, I compiled a list of tips. Many leaders and members have already found these tips to be helpful. Although all nine fruit of the Spirit should be exemplified in each situation, I broke down the list of tips, situations or ideas (somewhat randomly) so that each of them would fall under the category that at least seemed closest.

As you ingest the team concepts and devour the fruit of the Spirit, may this booklet be an appetizer to your full meal of spiritual potential and team growth. May the seeds that you plant (through your worship expressions and fruit-filled presentations) produce an abundant crop of healing, deliverance, and salvation.

Part One
Attitude Toward God & Team

Love, joy, and peace not only relate to our attitude toward God and how He relates to us with those characteristics, but if we allow Him to flow through us and also walk in the Spirit, we may likewise exemplify these attributes toward others.

Each of the definitions for the words love, joy, and peace, along with their supporting scriptures, speak so loudly in and of themselves that little expository is necessary. They can teach us a lot about how we should relate to God and our team.

The following team tips relate to prayer, being spiritually alert, rejoicing, and wholeness.

Chapter One
LOVE

Love An undefeatable benevolence and unconquerable goodwill that always seeks the highest good of the other person, no matter what he does.

*Romans 5:5 – Now hope does not disappoint, because the **love** of God has been poured out in our hearts by the Holy Spirit who was given to us.*

TIPS & TECHNIQUES

- Be willing to be spontaneous. Have spiritual acumen (sharpness, or quickness of understanding). During praise and worship, be aware of what is going on around you naturally and spiritually. Leaders—listen to the Spirit of God for changes in the service. Watch for directions from the leadership and worship director. Members—watch for the dance leader's directives. Be aware and on top of any changes the leader may give you.

- Fasting, prayer and Word studies are important to do both together and privately. Learn to hear the Father's heart for ministry during praise and worship as well as during presentation pieces. Up hold your dance leader and other dance team members in prayer, regularly. It is a good idea to study the Word not only on an individual basis, but also as a dance team. Study the meanings and scriptures associated with movement so you are aware of what you are doing while you dance for the Lord.

- Team members, don't burden the leader with complaints, concerns, or problems right before service. Praise the Lord right in the midst of your problems. Try not to mingle too much with the congregation before worship (if you have just come out of intercession or dance team prayer time). All this may be a deterrent or distraction from your time of ministry before the Lord.

- Watch choreographic pride (my dance—my choreography). It's all God's anyway. If choreography is purely conjured through the mind, then one can certainly understand where pride may enter the picture when someone else wants to use your work. However, if you are walking in the Spirit, and have prayed about the dance, then there should be no problem with others using what God has given you. I am tremendously blessed when others use the dances that the Lord gives me.

Since God is Love, and His love is shed abroad in our hearts, He will always seek the highest good for us no matter what we do. Then while we attempt to do His will, we too can share the love of God with others.

Chapter Two
JOY

Joy Rejoice, be glad, be joyful. To spin around with intense motion. Dancing or leaping for joy.

*Habakkuk 3:18 – Yet I will rejoice in the Lord, I will **joy** in the God of my salvation.*

Tips & Techniques

- We need to not only hold up the arms of our dance leaders, but also exhort, bless, and encourage those others who get chosen for certain special events or parts. Watch your heart attitude when someone gets chosen to do a certain part or to choreograph a certain dance for which you feel you should have been chosen. Get self out of the way. Rejoice with those who rejoice!

- Don't get upset when you are chosen to do "just flags" or "just cloths." It may be a test of your character, or the leader may need more experienced people to make sure that the flag part is done at the right time with good timing. It may be that the flag part is the most important part in the dance.

Just as God Himself rejoices and dances over us, so should we rejoice and be full of joy as we do His will. Even if our situations or circumstances seem miserable, we should joy in the God of our salvation. He will see us through!

Chapter Three
PEACE

Peace Completeness, wholeness, health, welfare, safety, soundness, tranquility, prosperity, fullness, rest, harmony; the absence of agitation or discord.

*Nahum 1:15 – Behold, on the mountains the feet of him who brings good tidings, who proclaims **peace!**...*

Tips & Techniques

- As a dance leader, know your place of authority and stand on it. Do not be intimidated by those more skilled then you. Come to practice with an air of confidence in the Lord. This avoids all the suggestions of people who only want to "help." Once the floor is opened up for suggestions, you may never get the dance practiced, because every one will have a *better* idea. Did they pray about the ideas? Was it their vision?

- Dance members, try to avoid helping too much. Let the leader work through the choreography. Sometimes it takes development and time. If you do make suggestions, be mindful of how they are presented. Perhaps seeing the leader after practice would be good.

- Leaders, during meeting times, re-emphasize and reassure the team that there are several different skill levels. Encourage them to participate in the dances at their own level and be comfortable with it.

- It may be a good idea to have three different levels of dances going at the same time or have three different levels within a particular dance. This will also raise up, activate, and stretch others to lead or choreograph. This may also give people a goal to stretch themselves with additional dance classes.

Be at peace with who you are as a person in Christ. If you are the called, chosen, appointed, and anointed dance leader, know that this is your place and stand in it. Like-

wise, have tranquility a
member learning to mov
level. Don't compare yo
room and place in the b
sound in their position
their own placement, t
tation or discord. Let
tain tops by first exp

Part Two
Social Relationships On & Off The Team

How do we act toward one another during practice times? Do we exercise patience with the team leader who is initially teaching new choreography? Do we exemplify goodness and kindness toward our fellow team members? How do we treat the new team member who can't quite pick up the steps or timing like everyone else? What about when we are with our family—do we show patience toward our small children when it would be easier "just to do it ourselves?" Do we show kindness to our teenagers after they just spoke unkindly to us? Do we show goodness toward our husband when on the inside, we may feel like he doesn't deserve it? Are we allowing Holy Spirit to do a work in our hearts so we may walk in the spirit and truly show by example this triad of fruit?

This section is devoted to defining patience, goodness, and kindness. With that, I trust you will get an introduction to their meaning and use this knowledge during social interaction both on and off the team. Also, you will have an acquisition of team tips that will be helpful in the days and years to come.

Chapter Four
PATIENCE

Patience "Long suffering, lenience, forbearance, fortitude, patient endurance, the ability to endure persecution and ill-treatment. It describes a person who has the power to exercise revenge but instead exercises restraint."

Hebrews 6:12 – *"That you do not become sluggish, but imitate those who through faith and **patience** inherit the promises."*

TIPS & TECHNIQUES

- Be flexible and willing to accept change and constructive criticism. Like 'Jell-O', a dance is not ready for presentation, ministry, or enjoyment until it is set. In the mean time, it is in an evolving process where we must exercise patience and understanding. One time, the Lord gave me a dance that had to be worked and reworked many times until we got it right. Every single practice we changed it just a little. This principle of patience and understanding came in handy, especially when everyone finally had it perfect at the last practice and I still changed another part. It was worth all the time and effort, though, because it truly ministered the heart of God.

- Don't strive for position or leadership. When it's obvious that you are striving for it, that is a sure sign to leadership that you are not ready for it. Be humble and submissive and serve *genuinely*. Be faithful in the little things (set up, clean up, etc.) with a loving attitude and eventually, (through patient endurance) you will be raised up. Check your heart motivation.

- Leaders be patient with your team members who are stepping out to try new choreography. It may take a while for people with little experience to pick up on a step right away. Give them lots of encouragement along the way, as they may feel somewhat awkward. Members, be patient with your leader who either gives you new choreography, new steps, or changes what you already have. Be willing to grow and be stretched. You will be blessed in the long run.

- If a leader makes announcements and/or changes and you are not specifically included; or if you are overlooked because the leader's focus may be on something else; or if you are not picked for a particular part that you thought you should have been, exercise restraint even though you have the power to exercise revenge. People (dancers especially) are often, somewhat egocentric. We tend to believe that everything revolves around us and when someone overlooks us, we tend to get offended. The truth is that leaders are human and they make mistakes. Primarily, however, their focus is on the dance as a whole and how it will minister to the Lord and the congregation.

We all need to exercise patience when it comes to working together as a team. We need to "imitate those who through faith and patience inherit the promises" (Heb. 6:12) and grant our leaders lenience while we exercise forbearance, fortitude, and patient endurance. If you accomplish this individually and inherit the promise, you may be the very catalyst of change who others imitate. Then, instead of there being a manifestation of grumbling and complaining, the whole team would be an awesome demonstration of patience, thereby inheriting the promises.

Chapter Five
GOODNESS

Goodness Kindness in actual manifestation, virtue equipped for action, a bountiful propensity both to will and to do what is good, intrinsic goodness producing a generosity and a God-like state or being. Combines being good and doing good.

Romans 15:14 – Now I myself am confident oncerning you, my brethren, that you also are full of **goodness**, *filled with all knowledge, able also to admonish one another.*

TIPS & TECHNIQUES

- Aim towards team unity. Work for the good of the team and the church as a whole. Work in conjunction with the worship team and leadership team. Be aware of what's going on in the service, naturally and spiritually. Don't get so caught up that you miss a corporate move.

- When someone is eventually raised up, anointed, and appointed to leadership, be willing to be submissive to and supportive of that person.

- Be willing to silently bring out or put away props. Will to do good especially without expecting reward or recognition.

- Offer to fold the cloths or wrap the flags or hang up the costumes. If you have the opportunity, and access, just do it without asking. Surprise your dance leader with a clean and organized wardrobe/prop closet.

- Just go in and clean the dance room mirrors. Sweep the floor. No one has to know that you were the one who did it.

- Create a computer-generated poster that relates to your team, focus, latest dance, etc., and put it up. Let them wonder who did it.

When you exemplify kindness in actual manifestation, and produce a generosity and Godlike state that combines being good and doing good, you will then be filled with goodness, all knowledge, and also, be able to admonish one another. This combination of both being good and doing good can each relate to people and deeds. If you initiate this kind of goodness with your team and behind the scenes, it will then be contagious. Others will begin to do the same. Menial tasks will not seem like a chore. The atmosphere of admonition will be "good" and the work load will be lighter for everyone!

Chapter Six

KINDNESS

Kindness Love for mankind, hospitality, readiness to help, human friendship, taking thought of others, lovingkindness toward men, goodness in action, sweetness of disposition, gentleness in dealing with others, benevolence, affability. The word describes the *ability to act for the welfare of those taxing your patience*. The Holy Spirit removes abrasive qualities from the character of one under His control.

Acts 28:2 – And the natives showed us unusual **kindness;** *for they kindled a fire and made us all welcome, because of the rain that was falling and because of the cold.*

TIPS & TECHNIQUES

- Respect the teacher or leader, even if you are more skilled. A humble, submissive attitude will get you a lot further then promotional expectations.

- Show hospitality by opening your home. Coordinate and hold a 'celebration' party after presenting a large production.

- Go out of your way to befriend someone who normally goes home alone. Usually, after a large production has been presented, the excitement level is high. If someone has to go home alone, (immediately afterward) sometimes depression will try to creep in. It is always good to fellowship for a little while.

- Help your leader out by taking extra time, on your own, to help someone on the team who doesn't understand some of the steps.

- Show lovingkindness to those team/family members who are, at times, not kind. They may have had a really hard day or life. Your simple act of kindness may crack their shell of insolence and, bring forth the deliverance they need.

- Don't wear your "heart on your shirtsleeve." Declare that: I will not receive an offense for any reason at any time!

Kindness and goodness are very similar to one another. However, kindness goes one step further. In addition to simply being good and doing good, kindness is an attribute that is described by the ability to act (or do good) for the *welfare of those taxing our patience.* Hurt people tend to hurt people. If we've been hurt in the past, it sometimes takes an extra measure of sweetness of disposition and gentleness in dealing with others for Holy Spirit to remove those abrasive qualities from our character. If we feel like someone "(sandpaper sister or brother)" has offended us, we need to think about how to handle it. Consider their heart motivation. Did they truly intend to hurt or was it simply our perception. Ask the Lord how to respond to the situation. When you respond with hospitality, lovingkindness and benevolence (instead of reacting with the works of the flesh), the result will be that of peace and harmony. When we allow ourselves to be under Holy Spirit's control, during all our social relationships, He will not only guide our behavior but also improve our character.

Part Three

Principles Guiding Conduct

In the Bible, we are given many types of roadmaps that guide the way we should live. The final three fruit of the spirit can be categorized as "principles that guide our Christian conduct."[2*] When we first get saved, there is often worldly residual in our lives. It is usually a process over a duration of time, that our conduct changes. Again, we must continually allow Holy Spirit to run our lives, by dying to the flesh, and submitting to His processes. How do we behave ourselves? Are we faithful to come to practice times? Do we keep our word? Are we gentle with one another? Are we able to control our tongue? If we follow these principles of: faithfulness, gentleness, and self-control, we will abound with blessings, be tranquil, and will be fruitful in the knowledge of our Lord Jesus Christ.

Chapter Seven
FAITHFULNESS

Faithfulness Firmness, stability, fidelity, conscientiousness, steadiness, certainty; that which is permanent, enduring, steadfast. To be firm, sure, established, and steady. Certain, stable unchangingly fixed.

*Proverbs 28:20 – A **faithful** man will abound with blessings, but he who hastens to be rich will not go unpunished.*

TIPS & TECHNIQUES

- We need to be continuously and conscientiously, available and on time. Promptness is important.

- If you are an advanced dancer, do not skip practices once you feel like YOU know the dance. Your leader needs you especially, to see how it all fits together. If you miss (and there were changes), then the leader has to spend extra time with you.

- Leaders, it may be good to set guidelines for required practice times.

- As the leader, show organizational effort by posting schedules for rehearsals, and clean up, etc.

- Take responsibility for your own attendance conduct. Have a date book for all rehearsals (in case of changes). Be sure you contact the leader or get back in touch if you've been away. Check the schedule regularly.

- Support and encourage your dance leader with a positive attitude and regular attendance.

- Be reliable, dependable, and eager to learn. Show a strong level of commitment.

We need to be people who are faithful in the little things. Then we will be given much. If we are reliable, dependable, steadfast, and enduring, without strife or striving, we will be given more responsibility. By virtue of this faithful conduct, the responsibility will not seem burdensome, beyond comprehension or ability. Steadfast servant-hood will bring much knowledge, understanding, and confidence in the area one is being faithful.

Chapter Eight

GENTLENESS

Gentleness A disposition that is even-tempered, tranquil, balanced in spirit, unpretentious, and that has the passions under control. Meekness (power and strength under control). The person who possesses this quality pardons injuries, corrects faults, and rules his own spirit well.

*1 Timothy 6:11 – But you, O man of God, flee these things (all kinds of evil) and pursue righteousness, godliness, faith, love, patience, **gentleness.***

TIPS & TECHNIQUES

- If the Lord gave you a vision, do not be swayed by suggestions that carry you in a different direction. On the other hand, do not discount other ideas that may enhance the vision (perhaps an area you did not see). Be even tempered, however, during your discussion.

- If someone does make a suggestion, be very gentle as to how you handle it. Their suggestion is often felt like it is a part of them. If you reject the suggestion, harshly, they may feel as if you are rejecting them. If you are gentle with them (handling their suggestion like a fine piece of china), you will be less likely to crush their spirit.

- Work on the part of the dance that you do have. Come at least partially prepared at practice even if you don't have the whole dance. This avoids confusion and the feeling of being "frazzled" or loose-ended. Be tranquil.

- Practice and complete a section during a practice time. This makes the team feel good—like they accomplished something (because they did!).

How we conduct ourselves is utmost. When we get shaken, what comes out? What is on the inside? If the works of the flesh come out, then we know it was 'in there'. We can not say, "I didn't mean to say that," or "That is not really how I feel." It *is* truly how we feel, if it is what comes out because we know, "out of the abundance of the heart, the mouth speaks." The good news is that during our Christian maturation process, God gives us principles that can guide our conduct in any given situation. If what is on the inside is not too pretty, we can temper what we say or do with gentleness. We can will to have our passions under control. We can pardon injuries, correct our own faults as they arise and rule our own spirit well. As we grow, we won't have to work as hard to 'will' gentleness, we will 'be' gentle and exemplify a disposition that is even tempered. Eventually, through our life long process, tranquility will be on the inside, replacing the works of the flesh, and we will be balanced in spirit.

Chapter Nine
SELF-CONTROL

Self-control To control of one's self, or of one's own emotions, desires, actions, etc.

*2 Peter 1:5-8 – But also for this very reason, giving all diligence, add to your faith virtue, to virtue knowledge, to knowledge self-control, to **self-control** perseverance, to perseverance godliness, to godliness brotherly kindness, and to brotherly kindness love. For if these things are yours and abound, you will be neither barren nor unfruitful in the knowledge of our Lord Jesus Christ.*

TIPS & TECHNIQUES

- Watch out for strife, jealousy, and competition!

- Don't draw attention to yourself. Be a part of the team (like a corps de ballet), or at least dance with the same "flow" as the leader.

- Never question or doubt what your leader says *(especially)* in front of the other team members. If your question is not answered by the end of practice, then quietly approach your leader on the side and pose the question or suggestion. Do not be offended if your suggestions are not always accepted.

- Use self-control to avoid gossip at all costs!

Have you ever noticed a small child who has boundless energy, and has had to sit quietly in a setting where it is inappropriate to 'wiggle'? Finally, when they can't take it any more, the wiggling commences. It then becomes a struggle between the parent who tries to exact self-control in the child, and the child who feels like they must continue wiggling. As Christian adults, we have the ability to control our own emotions, desires, actions, and wiggling tongue. Of course, we can do all things through Christ who strengthens us. For instance, we certainly do not have to gossip. Often, it is cloaked under the guise of prayer: "We really need to pray for sister Sally, did you hear what she did?" After all the gory details have been shared (in strictest confidence, of course) the prayer begins. The gory details are important, you know, so the prayers can be specific. The problem is, that once the "concern" gets out, people tend to look askance at that individual, until they feel alienated and rejected. If this happens to enough people, in sets bitter judgement and finally division. It is nothing but a downward spiral for families, teams within churches and the church structure itself. We as the body of Christ need to exhort, edify, and encourage one another, not tear down. We need to become a unified front against the enemy of our souls (not people). This unity can begin with the exercise of *self-control*. We *can* control the waggle of a tongue that wants to wiggle!

Conclusion

In order for us to have terrific teams, that exemplify the fruit of the Spirit, we must, not only adhere to good tips from experienced individuals, but also, die to our flesh, build up our spirit man and develop Christ-like-fruit-remaining character. When this process is successful, our arts presentations and worship expressions will then produce exemplary fruit of their own. They will leave a lasting impression of love, joy, peace, patience, goodness, kindness, gentleness, faithfulness, and self-control. As congregational onlookers are ultimately touched and changed, because of our growth, they, in turn, will affect another's life, and so on...

Bibliography

[1] * *Webster's New World Dictionary of the American Language*
All definitions throughout
Simon and Schuster, a division of Gulf and Western Corp. ©1982
1230 Avenue of the Americas
New York, New York 10020

[2] **Spirit Filled Life Bible – New King James Version*
All scriptures throughout and some comments
Thomas Nelson Publishers – Nashville
Atlanta – London – Vancouver
Thomas Nelson, Inc. ©1991
General Editor – Jack W. Hayford, Litt. D.
Old Testament Editor – Sam Middlebrook, D. Min.
New Testament Editor – Jerry Horner, Th.D.

Assistant Editor – Gary Mastdorf, M.S.

Mission Statement

Dancing For Him is a biblically based, spirit filled organization whose purpose is to minister healing and deliverance to people's hearts through creative expressions of worship, prophesy, and dance. As artistic ministers who transcribe the heart of God into an acceptable life changing form, we exist to teach others about this unique art form through which to spread the gospel of Jesus Christ and set captives free!

Dancing For Him Worship Dance conferences are only phase I of a Five-Phase plan. This is to: minister, train, and activate others to effectively reach the lost; heal the sick, wounded and broken hearted; and open prison doors to those who are bound. During these awe-inspiring conferences, technical dance training is obtained; but more important, an impartation of anointing to minister through music and dance is transmitted. Please visit our web site to see the other phases.

FOR FURTHER INFORMATION ABOUT:
- Attending one of our conferences
- Having us minister at your church
- Hosting a workshop in your area
- Getting on our mailing list

Please feel free to contact us at:

Dancing for Him Ministries, Inc.
Tom & Lynn Hayden
1 (800) 787-1623
info@dancingforhim.com
www.dancingforhim.com